A SONG FOR YOU

Marianne LaValle-Vincent

First Edition: 2020
Rs. 200/-

Cyberwit.net
HIG 45 Kaushambi Kunj, Kalindipuram
Allahabad - 211011 (U.P.) India
http://www.cyberwit.net
Tel: +(91) 9415091004 +(91) (532) 2552257
E-mail: info@cyberwit.net

Printed at Repro India Limited.

The album "A Song for You" by the Carpenters had special meaning for me back in the 70's. Each and every song on that track holds a memory that I cherish. But what I remember most, is that I shared the experience of listening to that album with one of my favorite people in the world—my sister, Weez! We must have played it 100 times, carefully analyzing each song and its hidden meanings and using a bit of psychology to apply the individual songs to our own lives.

I remember that the 70's weren't an easy time for me. It was the beginning of motherhood and the end of a marriage. It was a time of growth and a time of disappointment. It was a time that I discovered how deeply I could love another person, for nothing on this earth compares to the love I have for my three children. It was a time of loss. I said goodbye to my Mom and lost a piece of me that could never be replaced. I filled that void with whatever I could, but mostly I finally realized that my family was the key to my survival. My sisters gave me unlimited support, and my brother not only supported me (literally) but showed me how to embrace life with enthusiasm and success. I took 10 steps forward and 20 steps backward. I finally learned the value of education. I let go of my Pollyanna syndrome and got a lot tougher. I found love and lost it. I failed a hundred times but found success around the corner. And through it all, my family was there.

To my sisters and brother, I am eternally grateful. To my angelic parents, I miss you and want so much to make you proud. And to my children who have learned to do as I say and not as I did— congratulations; you are every Mother's dream. And to my future success stories—Brian, Joe, Mariana and Alivia:

This one's for you!

I know your image of me is what I hope to be
I've treated you unkindly but darlin can't you see
there's no one more important to me
baby can't you please see through me
cause we're alone now and I'm singin this song for you

I've acted out my life in stages
with 10,000 people watching
but we're alone now
and I'm singin this song for you

The Carpenters

Contents

THE RAZOR'S EDGE

that first time cut like a knife
I think I was 14 and I felt as if I were dying
his name was Mike and he was beautiful
he was my first kiss; my first love, my first heartbreak
he took me to a movie and held my hand
it was *West Side Story* and I was as memorized by the movie as I
was by him
about half way through the film he put his arm around me
I remember my heart beating so fast and hard I thought my chest
would burst
and I kept hoping I wasn't sweating
I had a baby blue shirt on and I was very concerned that I would
have pit stains
maybe I did
he never mentioned it
he walked me home and told me he loved me
it was almost as if I were floating
he called me every night and we would talk for hours
or at least until my Father told me to hang up
we met after school and walked together until the road took us in
different directions
and I felt alive and beautiful and special
and then it was over
just like that
no more phone calls—no more I love you
no more Mike
he was with her now
and I didn't realize then that it really wasn't an end
it was a beginning

of what would come to be
of heartache and misery
of reality and untruths
of a hundred million tears
and a thousand sleepless nights
it was then I discovered that love isn't always perfect
and that with every heartbreak we fight to heal
to survive and to start again
and you may think the scar named Mike has healed
yet for me it shall remain bloody and obvious
as if it were yesterday

***Young love comes at a time before the heart knows how to protect itself*

MUSIC MAN

I smoked my first joint with him
and he still doesn't know he took me higher than the weed
he took me a thousand feet in the air with his smile
and gave me a home on a cloud
he sang to me on a park bench
all the while looking into my eyes
and his voice was like silk yet it penetrated my soul
the music he spilled filled me with awe
and I believed in his rhythm
it was as if I lived in a pastel haze
for I could barely see past him
much less see through him
and I remember one night
after we smoked
I looked at him and he was the devil
and I remember wondering why I wasn't frightened
why I didn't care
he had my heart and my soul
and I was lost
he was my religion
until he found another disciple

I almost didn't come back after him
and it was near impossible to find myself again
I searched for an eternity for the girl that was
begging for acceptance from those that might notice
my limbs were broken along with my heart
and I couldn't hear the music
anymore

can you even imagine life without music
it is deafening
sometimes I remember the notes he sang
and I still pretend they were for me
I can hear them again but they will never
ever sound as sweet

****And those who were seen dancing were
thought to be insane*
by those who could not hear the music
Friederich Nietzsche

MIRROR MIRROR ON THE WALL

who's the fairest of them all
am I still able to turn a head
or am I simply better off dead
what of these wrinkles on my face
do you think anyone could embrace
the aged woman I've become
it's so hard to keep from being glum
and what of the twilight years ahead
should I accept being alone instead
I've so much to offer some lucky sweet man
but I want him to know this wasn't the plan
I never expected that at this age
it would be so difficult to turn the page
who knew the years would go so fast
and I'd be alone—why I'm aghast
I've still got it you know that much is true
but all this alone time is makin me cuckoo
so listen mirror don't play with my heart
show me that I can make a new start
turn back the years –how 'bout 45
ah those were the days so firm—so alive
erase those laugh lines it's not really funny
what will it take—shall I offer you money
to bring back the glow of a woman with spunk
instead of this gal who's deep in a funk
I'll make you an offer you just can't refuse
come on little mirror what could you loose
shine up your glass and erase all those years
make me look gorgeous and erase all my fears

are you ready my friend—I'll count to three
and when I look into you I'll be a younger me
one two three -—I'm ready Ms. Glass
are you even kidding you pain in the ass
nothing has changed I'm still 69
I believed in you—you're no friend of mine
I'd shatter you to pieces like an old sitting duck
yet the last thing I need is more friggin bad luck!

    ****Never look into a mirror if you are
afraid of the truth

THE QUARTERBACK

isn't it every cheerleader's dream to date the
quarterback
to live that age-old cliché
to be as bookends in the path of adolescence
hoping beyond hope that it'll be happily ever after
but what's hidden behind those uniforms
what happens when there are no masks
when the game is over
two children living a lie
crowd pleasing teens still fresh and innocent
hiding behind a reputation of glory
surrounded by a sense of false bravado
clinging to nothing but waiting for everything
the perfect high school couple
whose love never made it past high school
who went their separate ways never to meet again
was it just wasted time
or is it a memory that will forever remain in their hearts
were those pep talks something for the crowds
or were they words spoken by heroes in love
were they drawn to each other out of passion
or was it just something for the yearbook
a trophy duo
I think of him every once in a while
when I'm going through my old box of memoirs
I still have his fraternity pin
and my letter **S**
and even a few letters he wrote way back when
but mostly I have the memories of us

and they become better with the years that pass
so I choose to believe that we were the real thing
that all American twosome
who hid behind those uniforms
and pretended to be lovers
if only for a while

        ***You've gotta be a football hero to be in
love with a beautiful girl
            Rah rah sis boom bah!

AS PURE AS THE DRIVEN SLUSH

it's what happens when you're a late bloomer
when you're too naïve to see reality
when you still believe in fairy tales
you're trusting and honest
and empathetic and real
life is good
people are basically good
and no one is out to hurt you
and then you wake up
and you brush the dirt off
and kick away the deception
and the lies and the hurt
and you become hard
untrusting
a non-believer
a bitch
and people ask you why
but it's still too hard to talk about it
because you still feel like a fool
whose insides are exposed for all to see

it helps to swear
and to get angry
and you finally get that sex without love
isn't all bad
doesn't make you a whore
or leave you wearing a scarlet letter
and then you see that it's ok to be bad
every once in a while

to run with the sinners
they really are much more fun
but you're still hanging on to your heart
cause it's still in pieces
from when you thought the world was good

***To err is human—but it feels divine*
Mae West

I CAN READ YOUR MIND

I always knew you wouldn't stay
there was something in your eyes
something so far away about you
something mysterious
as if you were hiding the inevitable
even your most sincere lies
were just that
lies that I wanted so to believe
I always knew
you were unfaithful
that I was never your only love
and I wondered
if you loved them
as you loved me
did you tell them the same lies
promise them the same things
did they know about me
was I ever *the one*
and when it was over
you told me you were sorry
for not being able to love me the way I needed
you said you could never be enough for me
and I deserved more—
someone better
but that's not at all what you wanted to say
what you really meant is that I was never enough for you
and that you would never be happy with just me
Christ, you couldn't be happy with 50 women
and as I lie in this king size bed

I find no difficulty in adjusting to being alone
because I knew you would leave me
from the very first time you told me you'd stay

****His lies were so exquisite, I almost wept*
Dave Eggers

NOT SO TRANSPARENT

you thought you knew me
knew who I was
you were so sure you had me all
figured out
thought I was weak and vulnerable
yours for the taking
a feeble-minded girl who was lucky to
have you
but you never realized it was what I wanted you to
think
and in your perfect little world
I would never leave
I would be the faithful adoring
little woman
whose world revolved around you

ah how I loved your blindness
and how I took advantage of your ego
you mistook my silence for devotion
yet my only devotion was to myself
how I pretended to fall apart when you left
I played the victim so well
that you actually believed you hurt me
you thought you destroyed me

it must have been quite a shock for you
when you learned I didn't crumble
I survived
but I want you to know

I never would have left
at least not until I found someone better
because loving anyone
just isn't in the cards for me

Why fall in love and ruin each other???
It's too messy

JUST A LITTLE OFF KEY

we really never found our groove
he was mellow
        I was more upbeat
we just couldn't harmonize
and I always thought we were a little
flat
yet every once in a while
he'd surprise me with an unexpected
symphony
and sometimes he'd even earn an ovation
from me
if he was up for an overdue performance

but our music just didn't flow
it wasn't that we couldn't sing
or carry a tune
together
he just couldn't orchestrate an overture
and I couldn't relate to his score
so our music was just a little off key

we played together until the music died
and though it was sad
when he couldn't raise another encore
I remembered he always said he could never be
another *Bob Marley*
but I would have settled for
Notorious B.I.G.

        ***He was like a song I knew when I was a
kid—I forgot it till I heard it again*

A LOVELY AFTERTHOUGHT

I remember calling him whenever I was alone
he was reliable
and always available
he would joke about me not loving him
saying that someday
I would miss him
someday I'd wish he were mine
but I never worried about that
it was hard sometimes
to hurt him that way
yet he knew I would never feel
what he wanted me to
and I loved that he loved me
that he would do anything for me
and he accepted our
non-relationship
in such a way
that I almost pitied him
but not enough to leave him alone

I married
he never did
I divorced and he was still there
arms outstretched
heart wide open
his generosity overflowing
and one night I let him love me
and he was gentle
and adoring

and for just a little while
I may have loved him, too

I sobbed for a week when he died
not because I realized I loved him
but because I always knew no one would ever love me
like he did

        ***If he only knew how much I wanted to love
him——but I couldn't—I just couldn't

SUBLIMINAL

I'm unfinished
unformulated
a mystery
what you see is not always what you get
and I am
still hiding

I can be amazing
or ridiculous
sincere or
untrustworthy
gentle and loving
or brutally hurtful
and I am still
wide open

I am intelligent
and scatterbrained
intuitive
or naïve
generous and giving
or incredibly selfish
and I am still
unwritten

I struggle to write the next
chapter
and search for answers to questions
unasked

what will tomorrow bring
and what of all my yesterdays
is today all there is
how will my story end

and I remain
inexplicable

          ***I never tell anyone exactly how clever I am——
they would be too scared

TO THE MOON AND BACK

sometimes when the moon is in its
crescent form
I imagine myself sitting in the arc of that celestial body
legs dangling for all the world to see
searching the beauty in this earth
and as I seek out the majestic mountains
and the immeasurable oceans
hunt for the allure of the countryside
and the ever-present splendor of nature's
floral coasts
I am focused on a beauty most rare
a pure and radiant star
that shines ever brightly
for in the midst of this world's magnificence
there is for me a vision of radiance
breathtaking and mesmerizing
whose purity and devotion
has made me a believer in love
and all the beauty this world displays
pales by comparison
for when I search for perfection
in this incredible universe
I see only the world's most flawless creation
    you, my love
 I only have eyes for *you*

    ******My love must be some kind of blind love***
Are the stars out tonight——- I don't know if it's cloudy or bright
          The Flamingos

LaVALLE'S LAW

pack a picnic lunch
you can bet it'll pour
buy a new pair of shoes
I step in dog poo
and for sure if I try a new make-up
I'll have an allergic reaction
if I purchase a car
it'll probably be a lemon
win big on a scratchy
something in my home will need repair
and if I walk in the park
I'll most likely get mugged
go on a blind date
he'll be dressed in plaid
run in a marathon
you know I'd come in last
and if I even think of wearing stilettos
before the night's out—I'm gonna break a leg
but nothing stops me from trying
what's a few broken bones
or having to clean poo from brand new *Tamara Mellon* shoes
so I almost sever a digit when I'm chopping veggies
or trip over the dog and fall down the stairs
so what if the champagne cork almost pops my eye out
who's to say tomorrow won't be better—but
I'd be the gal to rip her *Dior* gown
definitely choke on an olive
and blow up like a balloon after eating sushi
maybe ruin a 150-dollar manicure

or accidentally break Bradley Cooper's nose
(if I were lucky enough to meet him)
but after all is said and done
I'm happy as all get out
and if I ever get my foot out of this wet cement
I'm gonna do a little dance to prove it!

****It's meeting the man of my dreams—*
then meeting his beautiful wife

Isn't it ironic??

Alanis Morissette

APOLOGY NOT ACCEPTED

I know there's holes in my
apology
and the scars I gave you
are still visible and fresh
please don't keep saying
you'll never forgive me
because somehow I think you mean it
this time
and it scares me
I don't know why I continue to hurt you
cause I can't imagine my life
without you
and after all this time
you must know I don't mean the things I say or do
but you say this time it's different
the hurt is too deep
you just can't get past it
but I know that can't be true
cause I see it in your eyes
I know you still love me
can't we start over
I promise I'll try harder
I'll give it my all
this time
please
just stay with me
give me one more chance
and as I watch you walk out the door
I'm breaking inside

but I can't say I'm sorry—not again
don't make me lie
for deep down we both know
if you should stay
I'll hurt you again

****Truth is—everyone's going to hurt*
you—you've just got to find the one
worth suffering for
Bob Marley

LOVE THE ONE YOU'RE WITH

don't we all settle at some point
for a secondary kind of love
that prince you waited for
never arrived on his white horse
but the construction worker
in the Chevy van
was a hell of a one night stand
and that handsome doctor
you dreamed about for all those years
never even gave you a second glance
hell—he married that skinny silicone boobed bimbo
30 years ago
yet a part of you still aches for that fantasy
and what about that drop-dead gorgeous
attorney
that handled your divorce
now he was a catch
but don't forget—
he was lousy in bed
what a waste

so here you are
in the arms of comfort
maybe not the passion you wanted
or the utopia you longed for
but you're safe and loved
and you're not alone
and as he kisses you good night
and you fall asleep in his arms

those age-old pipe dreams
fill your silly head—still
and you let yourself fall
into that fantastic hallucination
of true love—just one more time

*   ***If you can't be with the one you
love—love the one you're with*

UNINVITED

why are you here
you seriously think you can fix me
I'm not on the mend
and you need to understand
I don't want to heal
I don't need a champion
or a knight in shining armor
let me wallow in self-pity
for a little while longer
I'll let you know when I'm ready
to be rescued

you're not invited to this misery of mine
I never asked for a dose of your optimism
or your fatal attempts to save me
if you want to be with me
I need you to suffer
to hold on to my anguish and wretchedness
and to embrace my depression
as if it were your own
and if you can't handle that
then go away

you're not invited to my heartache
I'm not a damsel in distress
and you're not Robin Hood
I'm lost right now
not wanting to be found by you
or anyone else

not yet
the wounds he inflicted are still wide open
and I'm still bleeding
so instead of trying to be my band aid
why don't you help me convalesce
by bleeding a little yourself

          ***With the best intentions you throw me a life
line—but right now
            I'll just ignore it and probably drown. Save me later

PIANO MAN

I remember a million years ago
walking into that piano bar
smoke so thick with marijuana
you could get high just taking a breath
couples crouched over the old baby grand
hanging on to the crooner's every note
and he ruled that crowd
his voice was like nothing I ever heard before
deep and penetrating
and it invaded my soul
and he became my religion

for a time he sang only for me
and I lived in his unique rhythm
everything he wrote or played or sang
took me to a higher level
his music was mesmerizing
and I followed blindly
walking into the shadows
always behind him
    always a few bars behind
and then the smoke and the piano and the crowds
weren't enough for me
and though that life was his creed
I chose another sect
another path to the musical retribution
I said goodbye to his aria
and did a little a cappella

I miss that baby grand
and the man behind it
I still hear his voice and still imagine him
in that smoke filled joint
and I wonder who he's playing now

****Because when he sang—even the birds
stopped to listen*

ISN'T IT ROMANTIC?

it's a perfect evening to fall in love
the little hide-away restaurant
holds the perfect amount of ambiance
and the dimly lit room adds just a bit of mystery
he orders for you (which normally you'd object to
but it's a special occasion)
and his choices are right on
the conversation flows as if rehearsed
and he looks into your eyes at the exact moment
you were hoping for
the cocktails go down easily
and you're the right amount of tipsy
as he leans in for a kiss
it's exactly what you've been waiting for
only not from him
dessert is sensuous and exciting
and you enjoy the delicacy from the same dish
he hints of what's to follow
and you're immediately taken back to yesterday
yesterday when things were like a fairy tale
yesterday when love was all consuming and perfection
the stuff you read about
yesterday when *he* was sitting across from you
when all was right with the world
he takes you home and asks to come in for a drink
but you're tired and you're working tomorrow
he understands
but you don't
when will you understand

when do you get to move on
when do the memories fade
and when will your heart start to beat again
and you know you're only going through the motions of living
because any thoughts of romance died when he said goodbye

****I honestly have no idea how to live
without you*

Stephanie Meyer

SELF PORTRIAT

I'm just a Saturday kinda gal
stuck in a Monday world
goin through the week
like an animated ms. pac man
sometimes bumping into unseen obstacles
that seem to exist entirely for my
inconvenience
admittedly my music is a bit off tune
but I'm still dancing to it
and though I'm sometimes overwhelmed
with life
I'm still thrilled with it

and on those days when I'm stuck in that never changing
rut of the 9 – 5 grind
I listen to the music that takes me to Saturday
and it sooths me and gives me strength
and it fuels me with ambition and endurance
enough to face another gloomy week day

maybe this Saturday
I'll sleep a little later
cook something different
wear something outrageous
but I'll continue to play that ole-reliable tune
that makes it all fall into place
which is no small accomplishment
when you're a weekend kinda gal

****Love me like Saturday night—like three glasses of champagne*
Love me all weekend long

DANGEROUS

it's a dangerous man
that makes you believe
you can achieve the impossible
he can take you to the top of the mountains
or lead you to the hubs of hell
he can fill you with a passion you've never known
or crush you like an earthquake
and make you thank him for it
he'll make you a believer
in things you never knew existed
and you'll follow him
to places you know you shouldn't go
he's the light in a darkened room
an opening in the fog
he's a hurricane—a tornado
and the rainbow afterwards
he can pierce you with his words
and melt you with his eyes
he'll scar you with his promises
and you'll bleed his music and hemorrhage his lyrics
and his song will haunt for all the days to come
because dangerous is a way of life—it's who he is
and he offers no excuses—no apologies
his existence is for him and him alone
and he makes you feel dangerous, too
because he took you in
if only for a while
and when he's gone
you'll miss the perilous life

for nothing will taste as sweet
as his bite
nothing will satiate you like the wounds
he inflicted
and you'll search for that viperous partner
till you taste the blood again

****Things change when you're not in
danger anymore—it's boring*

WANT AD

the perfect partner wanted
please apply tout sweet
so tired of all these lonely nights
need a taste of a little male treat
must be willing to work overtime
evenings and weekends, too
you'll be highly compensated
but please don't misconstrue
you'll work at this position
like a soldier who's at war
I'm quite demanding and insistent
but I'm all that you could ask for

maybe we'll stay in bed one day
and sleep the time away
or perhaps explore a beach or two
we've so much time to play
expensive dinners and eclectic drinks
so much for us to do
beautiful clothes and rich sport cars
a perfect duo, who knew

so hurry and send that resume
I'm dying to meet the man
who'll give me all I'm longing for
and help me close the plan
but rest assured you'd better have
a bank account that's full
cause you'll be payin in more ways than one

and that, my love's—no bull

   ***Any woman who believes that the way to a man's heart is through his stomach—
      definitely flunked geography!

THEY SAY

they say everything happens for a reason
but I'm a doubter
can someone explain to me why you left
why I can't sleep unless you're holding me
is there any rhyme or reason to my refusing to accept your
decision
or waiting every minute of every day for a text or a call from you
what happened to all our plans for a future together
children and grandchildren—vacations and growing old
to love each other till the end of time
I truly believed in us—right from the beginning
so—-what the hell is the reason for *her*
she wasn't supposed to matter
she should have meant nothing to you
but you let her break us
is she prettier or smarter—a better lover or a gourmet cook
maybe she's thinner or has better hair
for the life of me I can't wrap my head around what happened
why I never saw it coming and why after all this time
I still don't understand
I search for you in every corner of my world
hoping to catch a glimpse of your beautiful face in the grocery
store or the mall
I have a constant death grip on my cell
for fear I'll miss a call from you
and at night when I'm crying in my bed alone
I find comfort in the fact that you never returned my keys
and maybe you'll just come back home one of these days

they say time heals all wounds
but what if time stands still
what then
I can't see past us
and I can't find any reason to believe things will get better
if it's always going to be
me without you

****If you'd told me before it would have
been a reason—but tell me after the
fact, and it's an excuse*

Carlos Wallace

BLUE MOON

I'm standing on the ocean bank
moonlight bouncing off the water
and staring into that crystal-clear sea
I imagine your face
staring back at me
beckoning me to join you
you're smiling and happy
and I remember those days
picnics on the beach
loving you in the sand
the luminous waves crashing into our bodies
warm and sensual
and we were everything
we were the sun and the moon
and the sky
we threatened to outshine the moon and the stars
and even the depth of that water
wasn't as profound as our love

and then we were no more
the moon and the stars outshone us
and the ocean claimed you for its own
and I am left with the only that blue moon
that used to light our way

and as I feel the ocean's strength
slowly engulfing me
taking me under
I brace myself for the inevitable

reunion
and reach for your hand
and that blue moon promises to take me to you
at last

      ***Blue Moon—now I'm no longer alone—
without a dream in my heart

Without a love of my own

SLEEPLESS IN SYRACUSE

the television whispers re-runs of *Golden Girls* and *Frasier*
as I mindlessly drift through Facebook
not really reading anything and mostly hoping for sleep
the dog snores at the foot of the bed
and I wonder if he knows how lucky he is
not a care in the world
unlike me who at this point in time
seems to be carrying the weight of the world
numbers fill my head as I absent-mindedly
try to balance my checking account without looking at it
suddenly a memory of what happened earlier in the day aggra-
vates me again
and I feel the anger rise
that passes quickly and I check my phone for the time
it's 4:44 am
now I'm flooded with memories of my daughter's birth
since she was born at that exact time
I stay in that memory for a moment and then it's on to work
related trivia
I focus on what has to be done when I get into the office
it's 5 am
I have to be up in about 2 hours
now I can't remember if I set the alarm
I check my phone—it's set
suddenly I'm on a sandy beach in Cancun
I'm walking rather quickly and not enjoying it at all
I hate the sand
and I'm not overly fond of the ocean
there's lots of colorful umbrellas and gorgeous native men

I'm running now because I'm late but late for what?
I'm checking my watch when the white rabbit appears
he tells me to hurry——*you have to hurry*
the alarm brings me back to earth and I bolt out of bed
I'm at the office not really knowing how the hell I got here
and surprisingly enough—I'm not tired
I check over my shoulder for the white rabbit—he's gone
but why the hell do I have sand in my shoes?

****All that we see or seem is but a dream within a dream*

Edgar Allan Poe

TO BEE OR NOT TO BE!

it was a cold January night
I think it was our second date
we were on our way to a party when the heater in his car died
we pulled over on the parkway and talked
there were no cell phones back then
I guess he figured if the car rested for a while
we might get some heat when he started it up again
he lit a cigarette and asked me about my future
and I remember thinking that he was kinda weird
so why the hell did I agree to go on a second date with him
the heat never worked again and it was a long drive to his friend's
house
we decided to pass on the party and he took me home
that night was a turning point for me

I never saw that boy again
and I finally understood that it was ok to aim for the sky
maybe I'd never reach the moon, but I sure as hell would grab a
few stars along the way
and I've grabbed more than my share
I've never been afraid to take a chance
never been afraid of rejection
I've made a million mistakes and learned a lesson from each and
every one of them
I've embraced this life and never ran from a challenge
loved like crazy and broke a few hearts
had my heart ripped out more times than I care to admit
but I wouldn't trade the experiences for anything
and I learned that the weirdos are *awesome*

the people that don't fit in are the best of the best
they make the world stand up on its axel and take notice
and I'm happy to say I've been blessed to spend time with some
of them
hell, I am one of them

so here's to never settling
here's to the artists and the musicians and the writers
here's to those special weirdos like me and that boy
may we both continue to experience everything this world has to
offer

****To be successful, you have to be one of three
bees: The queen bee, the bee
        that works the hardest or the bee that just doesn't
fit in! I've been all three*

NUMB

it was 6:30 on a Tuesday evening
we sat at the kitchen table and you held my hand
I can still remember the room spinning
your voice barely audible as you told me of her
how you tried to fight it
    and you never wanted this to happen
        you never wanted to leave me
I couldn't speak
I was totally emotionless totally dazed
numb
incapable of speaking I stared into nothingness
trying to hate you wanting to lash out
but I couldn't move *I couldn't even cry*
and I watched you walk away as if you were disappearing
into a never-ending abyss
leaving me to find a way out of a depression so deep
even taking a breath was painful

fast forward 2 years
I'm sitting at that same kitchen table
still surrounded by your memory
I force myself to breathe
but it still hurts
some nights I crawl into bed and can't remember anything
did I work today
did I eat
why did I bother to wake up
you still haunt my dreams and invade my mind

and I can't remember the last time I laughed
I mean a real laugh—not something for the crowd

I don't pray to feel anything anymore
because I realize this numbness is why I'm still surviving
cause I know I'd never make it
if I could still feel the love

       ****Better to feel nothing—to be numb—than to*
lose control
        It's the only way I can deal with the loss

THE ROAD TO NOWHERE

it's been three years, 67 days, 13 hours and 42 minutes
and I'm still hoping
still waiting for you to love me enough
still praying for that miracle
maybe I should be satisfied
with you as my lover
satisfied that you're in my bed
happy that I'm not always alone
but it's your eyes—*it's in your eyes*
that void
        that empty look that leaves me on the road to nowhere
and I'm stranded
do I turn around and start again with someone new
or do I keep on the same path
walking with you to the end of the road
never knowing if you'll be there with me
or if you'll suddenly make a U turn
forcing me to take another route
without you

and if it's the end of the road
I don't know if I can handle it
because every turn
        every detour
                every change of direction
has led me back to you

this road we're on is so familiar now
so well-traveled are we

so comfortable with our familiarity
but what I wouldn't give to know where it will lead

       ***A good traveler has no fixed plans
and is not intent on arriving
           I never did travel well

WHITE RABBIT (FANTASY)

one pill makes you smarter
and one pill makes you cool
and the ones that cost more money
make you feel like you're a fool
just ask Alice
      when she's miniscule

and I love to chase that rabbit
when he's nesting in my head
cause the medicine he gives me
is everything he said
go ask Alice
      when she's almost dead

and the queen can take your head off
but you'll never feel a thing
for the chessboard has you running
like the king's little plaything
just ask that rabbit
      that you're worshipping

when logic and understanding
have finally disappeared
and the magic jack of diamonds
has finally volunteered
to be your knight in armor
and never leave your mind
hold that rabbit
cause his love is blind
      ****Feed your head! Feed your head!*

I HAD TOO MUCH TO DREAM

my head is swimming
I'm in kind of a purple haze and I don't want to be awakened
it's so real
you're here with me again
and we're laughing
you're sitting on the hood of your 1965 *Corvette*
smoking a cigarette
your black hair shinning in the sunlight
telling me that same old joke
and I'm so happy—*but you're not*
you take me in your arms and I can feel your hot breath
and I remember what you tasted like
I can smell your cologne and it's intoxicating
why aren't you happy
you've got that god damn gun in your hand
and I'm scared
I'm so frightened
Jesus, I'd rather you pointed it at me
I need someone to wake me
cause this isn't a dream
anymore
it's a nightmare
and I know how it ends
and I can't bare to face it again
please don't make me face this horror again

I'm struggling to catch my breath and my heart's racing
and the vision of what you did floods my brain
and I search the inside of my soul for a reason
why?

I sleep with the light on for the rest of the night
and though I'd give anything for your return
I'd rather remember you in my dreams *as you were*
than face the reality of your demise when I'm awake

>   ***Why didn't you have the courage to* *live?? Anyone can die*

A SONG FOR YOU

searching for god knows what
been around the world a hundred times
or more
broke all the rules
made a million mistakes
and still: *here you are*
I try so hard to be what you want me to be
but it never works
my restless soul keeps running
afraid of being in one place for too long
never relaxed
and I keep trying to find answers
in people and places
that promise me everything
and give me nothing
yet you're still here
why is it you see in me what I hope to be
but I'm still reaching for those unattainable goals
never feeling quite good enough
    never good enough

and I love you like bread
and I don't know why I keep fighting
cause maybe you really are every answer
and I don't know why I'm afraid of you
or maybe it's cause I'm just afraid of us

my song is unfinished—out of tune
but please believe me

it's only for you
I can't sing it—-*not yet*
cause I just can't make the music sound like it should
until I learn to love myself

   ***I think I spend too much time trying to*
fit in cause I was meant to stand out

WHAT DO YOU MEAN

I tell you to go
but beg you to stay
tell you I want you
then push you away
start a fight
and call you names
pretend I don't care
and say you're to blame
it's complicated
you n me
enemies during the day
lovers at night
you turn to the left
and I pull right
I hate you on tuesday
and love you wednesday night   *what do I mean*
and if I really am what you're looking for   *what do you mean*
when you say you need time
I'm not a machine
turn me off
turn me inside out
tonight you're hurtful
tomorrow a boy scout
love me or leave me
but make me want to stay
love me 2 times boy
like that old cliché   *what do you mean*
it's a circus with us
all three rings wide open

nothing to discuss
stuck here with you
but I don't wanna leave
stuck in this mind trap
and yet I believe
I mean it when I say
I think I might love you

***If I choose you forever, can I change my mind?

NEVER, NEVERLAND

I was a child when I met Peter
he taught me to fly and dream
and valuable lessons about being
young at heart
and together we discovered
the joys of our youth
with just a bit of help from the fairies
and though I clung to his shadow
and tried to follow
my youth slipped away from me
that naïve little girl that lived in a
make-believe world
grew and grew
until she no longer had a need
for Peter or his narcistic life
and try as I might
fighting to remain innocent
I became an adult
much to Peter's chagrin
and just as I knew he would
he flew away
leaving me with memories
of a childhood gone too soon
and now when I think of him
and those flights of fantasy we took
I wonder how it all happened so fast
and I ask myself every single day
how Peter can still be such a child

how he can still refuse to mature
for I am the one with the responsibilities
while he continues to chase the fairies
and when he returns to have me sew his shadow on
for the millionth time
perhaps I'll leave it a bit on the loose side
so he can have room to grow

I am youth—I am joy—I am freedom
Peter Pan

ENIGMA

I love white
but always wear black
hate the rain
but won't go out in the sun
caught the never-ending dream
but purposely let it slip away
and in the middle of nowhere
I am not lonely
yet lost in the crowd
I ache from being alone
and I found you
after a rainy day
and wrapped you in the shelter of my heart
never letting you see the light
for I was afraid you would like it
and you would leave the darkness of my soul behind
like so many others before you
and I hate that I love you so much
and I love that you hate being trapped
for it is the power of my very being
to keep you to myself
never sharing your talents or your songs
and in spite of my independence
I am dependent on you for breath

I run to you
yet fly away in fear
and if I give in to you
I take more than I should

for if I were to show you who I really am
you would run from the reality
and I would be forced to live in a world
where the sun shines every day

****I am an enigma, wrapped in a dilemma,
surrounded by a conundrum*
Nanette Mathews

LOVE, BIPOLAR

I'm up
you're down
you're in
I'm out
don't really want to go
but not into staying
love you on Monday
forgot you on Wednesday
needed you yesterday
ignoring you today
you're happy
I'm sad
you're sad
I'm ecstatic
leave me alone
but take me with you
kiss me goodbye
but please never go
love me tonight
like I'm the only one
but like me in the morning
when I push you away
understand my insecurities
because I don't
and when I'm through with you
and tell you it's over
hold me like there's no other choice
and I'll fall in love again
I'll bury my head in the strength of your love

and pretend you're the weak one
and maybe tomorrow I'll be there for you
but only if I'm in the mood
to leave

    ****Somewhere between love and hate lies confusion. It's where I live*

HOLY ROLLER

she bows her head and prays—
prays for the repose of her soul
takes communion and says the rosary
after mass she meets her married lover
free from guilt or remorse
she volunteers for the salvation army
helps to feed the poor
and helps herself to a few bucks she feels no one will miss
late at night she falls to her knees
looks to the heavens for guidance
and tries to justify her transgressions
her dreams are full of apologies
though she lusts for a richer life
and she plays the role of a Christian
because it makes her feel less soiled
she lies when it's convenient
pretends a righteous existence
and at times she almost sees the halo she's imagined she's earned
Tuesday evening choir practice
followed by a Wednesday morning deception
and the people she fools follow like sheep
for the image she projects has been perfected
by her inequities and shortcomings
she sits in the front pew of St. Cecelia's
her back to the congregation
stares at the altar in utter defiance
and prays like it's her job
and she waits for the miracle she thinks she deserves
just like every other godless sinner

and she'll continue to pray and ask his forgiveness
but she is who she is
she just can't change
but you see—it's ok—-*she's religious*

                    ***Anyone who thinks sitting in church*
can make you a Christian
                    must also believe sitting in a garage can
make you a car

I WILL SURVIVE

the door slams and I feel myself exhale
there it goes
23 years of marriage
of children and family
of love and romance
turned to indifference and sarcasm
23 years of hopes and dreams
turned nightmarish and bleak
and I cringe at what tomorrow may bring
I don't even realize I'm crying
I'm so used to the tears they seem to just flow
without rhyme or reason

3 bedrooms
1 person and a house full of nothing
make for a lonely evening
pouring a glass of wine I remember the younger me
fearless and ambitious
unstoppable
and I think of what I've accomplished
in spite of him———*in spite of her*
somewhere that girl is still in there
and after all the dirt
the name calling and smut
that girl is still fighting to survive
still hanging on

it's an incredible awakening
when you come to the realization that you're gonna make it

I'm gonna live another hundred years without that son of a bitch
and this time around
it's finally gonna be about me

> ***At first I was afraid I was petrified—*
kept thinkin I could never live
> *without him by my side*......I will survive!

PUNCTUATION

this morning will be followed by a comma
perhaps the story continuing into the evening
with emphasis on the date I have scheduled
{gasp}
hoping for a bunch of exclamation points
I face the night head on—no need for a pause
yet full of question marks and hyphens
lots of quotation marks fill the void
and the wine increases the level of interest
he tells of his accomplishments
with interjections and apostrophes
and perhaps a smiley face here and there
at this point if I were an emoji
I would be a heart with an arrow through it
colored blush for all the world to see
and we dance
with more question marks hanging in the balance
time passes with colons on the digital clock
and we find ourselves alone
in a mysterious shroud of possibilities
not ready to say goodbye
but hesitant to enter another level
and up pop those pesky parenthesis (what should I do)
well…..(ellipsis) hyphen—what the hell

and afterward I'm thrilled—exclamation point
it was all I'd hoped for—another exclamation point
and now I'll sleep and dream the dream of lovers

semi colon—-until he loves me another time
period

   ****I want to change my punctuation. I long for excla-
mation marks but I'm drowning in ellipsis*

LOVER

drowning in self-pity, you found me
exactly the life jacket I needed
head barely above water I struggled to be
to exist after my destruction
and you helped me reinvent myself
helped me find a way
to go on
and you loved me to perfection
and you loved me back to reality
and though my self-destructive ways
tried to prevail
you filled me with answers
to questions I was afraid to ask
and it was the way I needed to be loved
back then
so pure and unselfish
it was a love that sustained me
a love that was nourishment
like bread
    like water

and I loved you as best I could
for someone who had no heart
and I gave you all I had
but there was so little left to give
you had to go——*I know*
you had to survive
for all I could offer would never be enough

I think of you on Sundays
when you used to bring me lily of the valley
and I inhale your memory
God, I hope you're happy with her
and I hope you know
how much I tried
to love you

****When you are drowning in lies, truth is
your only lifeline*

THE WAY WE WERE

I sit back and admire the living room
new furniture
　　　new wall art
　　　　　　fresh flowers
the dining room table shines with pride
inviting and warm
ready and waiting for a dinner party to happen
each and every corner decorated to perfection
and I bask in the newness of my home
inhaling the scent of tomorrow
but I remember
that old green sofa and wooden rocker
where we sat and toasted our future
our future that never came to be
our future that was squashed by lies and deceit
I still hear the laughter of the children
as they chased the dog in circles around the house
and the music from the old piano played a happy tune
I can smell the aroma of happiness and contentment
but it's missing, now
the house is lovely and quiet and untouched
but it's lonely and empty
and though it's decorated to perfection
it lacks that certain feeling
I think it was love

I pour a glass of chardonnay
using my very best *Versace* glass
try to ignore that it just doesn't taste quite as good as before

and close my eyes to go back to another time
when a *Corona*
right out of the bottle
and you by my side
was all I ever needed

*****You'll never find anyone as good for you as
I am, to believe in you as much*
as I do or love you as much
Barbra Streisand as Katie in "The
Way We Were"

CHANCES ARE

you said
take a chance on me
and I did
I dove into your lies
made a religion of your deception
and found a reason to believe
you washed over me like a torrential rain
erasing what I was
what I wanted to be
and the deluge of your storm
left me weak and broken
and you kept at me
like waves in a hurricane
destroying anything in your path
any hope for survival
    any chance for air
and then you were gone
and I cried
but not for you
I wept because I was free
free to start again
to regain my lost strength
almost like a rebirth
and chances are you'll never know
how I lost myself in you
and I'm sure
you never thought I'd survive
the tempest that you created
the destruction that you caused

I flaunt my scars proudly
now
they are my badges
and they will always remind me
of what I'm truly capable of

****Chances are you believe the stars that
fill the skies are here in my eyes*
                                    Johnny Mathis

MEMORY LAPSE

I keep forgetting
we're not in love anymore
because I can't bring myself
to get rid of the clothes you left behind
or your coffee mug
     or your slippers
I keep forgetting
you don't live here anymore
because I still feel your presence
still smell your aftershave
and the key chain that you placed on the dresser
the night you left
is still in the same spot
I keep forgetting
you're with her now
because my heart still won't believe it
and I still can't bear the thought of you with someone else
you're gone

I keep forgetting to water the plants
and even though they're slowing dying
I find comfort in their wilted leaves
like kindred spirits we are
and perhaps I purposely refuse to water them
for misery loves company
their emaciated branches
remind me that with just a bit of water
they will be ok
     they will survive

as I will
with just the memories of you
yet I keep forgetting
you don't love me anymore
but how vividly I remember
I can't love you any less

****Every night I lose sleep thinking of you sleeping in her arms*

BELIEVER

I believe in the power of God
and the kindness of strangers
I believe in family—in the importance of Sunday dinners
in the celebration of birthdays and other extraordinary milestones
I believe in the future of my grandchildren for their capabilities are
limitless
I believe in education—
not just from books and universities, but from hard work and the
observance of other cultures
from those who do wrong as well as those who always do the
right thing
education from politicians whose ignorance speaks volumes
and from clergy whose sins have been made public
I believe in the magic of the moon and the breathtaking vision of
the sunset
I believe in second chances and sometimes even a third or fourth
and I believe that the power of a memory
can bring you to your knees
I believe in angels and their significance
and I, unfortunately, believe in Satan
for I can find no other explanation in the deterioration of our
society
I still believe in falling in love—wildly, deeply and forever
in relationships and marriage—passionate love affairs and long,
soulful kisses
I believe in the comfort of a best friend
the strength of a sibling and the unconditional love given by a
parent
I believe that there is no greater love than the love for ones' child

and that I have been blessed to the moon and back with children
that may change the world
I believe in myself
in what I have accomplished
in the obstacles I have overcome and in what I have yet to
achieve
I believe tomorrow will be a better day
that yesterday is over and we must learn from it
and I believe in prayer
for it has seen me through the unimaginable that I foolishly
believed could never happen
finally, I believe in the future
for it holds the answers to all our questions
and I believe—with all my heart and soul—
that what awaits me— *my destiny*
will be nothing short of incredible

****Remember—the future depends on what you do today*
Mahatma Gandhi

WARRIOR

To my friend, Jean with a hopeful heart

it's just another morning
maybe a bit on the gloomy side
thinking of all I want to do
I smile in anticipation of the day
and then I remember
things are different
for 70 years my body has been a friend
and now
for no apparent reason
it's turned on me
it's broken
it's diseased
who let this monster in?
and why me?
controlling the fear is no easy task
but I'm trying
trying to hide my mortality
my reality
and friends try even harder
to ignore the dreadful diagnosis
don't say the word
don't ask any questions
just tilt your head to the side and tell me
it's gonna be ok——is it?
how the hell do they know—I don't even know what's going on
inside me
and I imagine myself as a warrior

fighting the battle of my life
good against evil
hoping for the phenomenon of modern medicine
a miracle
I am not the same—I am a cancer victim
and after the fight of my life
we can talk again
about how I survived
this dreaded enemy
and lived the rest of my life
like I was dying

****Cancer may have started the fight—but I sure
as hell will finish it!

STAND BACK

the time was right
for me to follow
yet I couldn't let you lead
not content to walk beside you
I tried to show you my way
but you couldn't stand back
you couldn't let me blaze the
trail
and the competition grew heated
and your negative attention was more than I could do
if you could just *stand back*
just give me some space
I wouldn't have walked too far ahead
just far enough to flaunt my
independence
but you wouldn't give in
you just refused to stand back

fast forward a few tears
and I'm walking ahead of everyone
but I'm walking solo
no competition
and he asks me if it was worth the price
this independent thing
and I look into his eyes
and tell him how hard it was
to become who I am today
it's hard to be alone
maybe we could have worked it out

eventually
maybe I would have walked beside you
after a little while
if you would have let me take the lead
just once

stand back—stand back—in the middle of my room
I did not hear from you———-like a willow I can bend
Stevie Nicks

SPINNING

sometimes the world spins out of control
and the axel tilts a little too far left
we hold on for dear life
but eventually we fall——-hard
we know the answer is to climb back on
but it's just spinning too fast
and it hurts to try
the climb back on is rough
we're battered and bruised and our confidence is shattered
we're grasping at the fantasy but reality pulls us hard
and the world just keeps spinning
like a carnival ride we never bought a ticket for
and everything we knew—everything we counted on
has fallen off the ends of the earth
up is down and west is east
time flies as if it were threatened
and the sun hides behind the moon like an intimidated lamb
but we keep trying to jump back on that spinning axel
and then one day it all starts to make sense again
time is on our side and the stars are in perfect alignment
love songs make sense again and we grab on to the fantasy
holding tightly as is humanly possible
because this time it's real
this time it's going to last
and all is right with the world——for now
but that axel will spin out of control again
you can count on it
and we'll fall — maybe even harder next time
and as we spiral down once more

maybe you'll hold on a bit tighter this time
maybe your days won't be nights
and you won't have two left feet or cry at coke commercials
but I doubt it
because love is always out of control
it's never as the poets claim
it's a road paved with thorns and you're driving blindly
but, oh! When the ride is smooth—when the axel spins perfectly
there's nothing better in this world!

      ***If you're emotionally unstable—can't put a
sentence together—can't eat or sleep
      and you're nauseous all the time—congratula-
tions!!! You're in love

CRAZY MOON

ah—the things that silvery orb can make me do
just a hint of its radiance can send my heart racing
and oh! when it's full I fall in love all over again
and that little man that makes a home way up there
sends me messages throughout the night
for only his magical sphere can drown out the brightest star
sometimes I'm coaxed into madness
for even that crazy moon has a dark side
and it lulls me into its light
and like a fool I try to embrace it
only to make it disappear until its once again ready
to make another brief appearance
and though that brilliant ball sometimes changes shapes
it is a constant promise of another night to come
a forever reminder that other lovers are witness to its glory
and a heavenly glow when there is only darkness

oh how I long to walk among the stars and live on the moon
for I imagine the moon is only for those madly in love
and I will find you there——waiting
the moon will be in quarter shape when I arrive
for that is my favorite
and you will be sitting on the edge
hanging on to a star
that you plucked from the sky just for me
and in the light of that moon you will once again love me
for it's impossible not to be in love
when you've been moonstruck *again*

****Love don't make things nice—it ruins every-
thing and breaks your heart!*

It makes things a mess! It ain't perfect— only
the snowflakes are perfect!

Ronnie Cammareri in Moonstruck

JUST FRIENDS

you say you remember
the way things used to be
they're such great memories
we had fun, didn't we
and I wish I could have seen your eyes at that moment
eyes that lied to me—eyes that couldn't see who I was
way back then
fun? you think it was fun?
did you know that each time I watched you walk away I died a
little bit
you think I didn't know I meant nothing to you
that your lovemaking was rehearsed and empty
and your self-indulgence was at my expense
how amusing I must have been to such a skilled seducer

well, I find it amusing now—a million tears later
you calling me your friend
you text me and say you made a mistake way back then
you just didn't know what you had
but I knew——I always knew what you had
and the mistake was mine, my part-time lover
because I used to think you were really something
I used to think it was my loss
and each time you left me—alone and wounded from your neglect
I wondered why you couldn't love me
why you wouldn't love me
but it's all so clear now, *my friend*
and it's amazing to me how time can heal

heal those bleeding wounds that you had no trouble inflicting, *my
friend*
you were never more than a fleeting moment in time
a stepping stone on my way up
for when I lost you— I found something amazing
something wonderful and exquisite
I found me
so I wish you happiness——honest I do
but most of all I wish you a friend like you were to me

       *****Two friends drifted apart—two friends but
only one broken heart*
               Just friends—lovers no more

BROKEN WINGS

I stopped to help a tiny bird who had fallen from his nest
his wing was obviously injured and he was crying in pain
yet when I reached out to comfort him
he pulled away
his fear of human touch was stronger than his desire to be free of pain
and I wondered if perhaps he had been hurt before
if that ever so helpless creature had once been abused by some-
one he loved
leaving him so broken and so full of fear
that he would rather suffer than put his trust in another human
and I thought of you
    and how you broke me
and the pain came again in turbulent waves
and I remembered how long I suffered alone and silent
trying to heal myself from the bitter sting of your abuse
refusing help from anyone for fear I would hurt like before
and my vulnerability remained for all the world to see
and I became almost impenetrable
living in unfluctuating fear of human contact
of another heartbreak
    or another love that could leave me bleeding again

and so—though I was broken and fragmented
I entered the world again—slowly and deliberately
with uncertainty at first
and with trepidation much like that tiny bird
I spread my wings and learned to fly again
and I was astounded by my strength
aching in anticipation of love and affection

and I found it—- almost purposefully
embracing the sentiment as if it were bread or water

I picked up the little bird
he resisted and fought a bit at first
but slowly he trusted me and he stayed until he healed
and when he was well enough to leave
I whispered to him *"if you doubt you can fly—you will surely
cease to do it"*
and he spread his wings and headed towards the heavens
taking pieces of me with him on his flight to his future

*****Said Oz to the tin man: You are in luck not
to have a heart—*
For someday, it will surely break

GOODBYE

I know you're not coming back
not this time
and I wonder how I'll get by
what will I do with my evenings?
evenings that have become an eternity
sleepless nights alone in a bed too big for one
how will I face tomorrow or the change in seasons?
who will ask about my day or lock the doors at night?
I remember when you loved me
when we were so happy with so little
we danced down that primrose path never looking back
but I guess we didn't really look ahead, either
and together we became successful and much too comfortable
for though the struggle was over
our triumphs were short lived
and being at the top wasn't all it was cracked up to be
I wanted to make it work
but you wouldn't work at saving us
and we crumbled—like clay
falling into so many pieces
we were impossible to put back together

so you tell me goodbye
and I'm barely breathing
I look into your eyes searching for the warmth that drew me to
you
but I find nothing but an icy cold stare
and as you turn and walk away
I whisper that I still love you—-*I always will*

and you quickly respond: *love somebody else*
and I want to——*God, I so want to*
and maybe one of these days I'll learn to love again
maybe I'll survive this horrid break
but until then
I'll start by trying to hate everything about you
because it's the only friggin way for me to get through this

    *****I hope you go to hell———I hear it's particularly nice this time of year*

DÉJÀ VU

I seem to be surrounded by familiar faces and feelings
an overwhelming sense of uneasiness
fills me with memories of what's going to happen
and I find myself falling into a sort of rabbit hole
I'm half expecting the *Mad Hatter* to appear and I search
for anything that will help me remember
it's incredibly dark and it's starting to rain yet I feel no fear
for there in the blackness I see you——finally and at last
your face and body are perfect with no signs of scars
and the green in your eyes tell me I'm safe
but safe from what
because it was never me that was in danger
and the only real danger you felt was the fear of tomorrow
the unrelenting fear that you couldn't take the pain
that you weren't good enough
     or strong enough
          or well enough to withstand life
and I try to run towards you but I'm motionless
my legs are too heavy and I just can't go forward
but I know what you'll do if I don't stop you
because this dream is recurring and I know how it ends
and then the *White Rabbit* tells me to hurry because he's late
I'm late
and I want to save you from yourself but *Alice* tells me if I try
the *Queen of Hearts* will cut off my head
and then suddenly I'm nothing more than a pawn in the chess
game
and I can't find you
I'm calling out your name and I'm pleading with you to answer

but the smoke from the *Caterpillar's* hookah has filled the hole
and I can't see
the chess board seems to have me glued in place and the
Cheshire Cat
is attempting to tell me what the hell is happening
since he is the only one with any sense of logic
he tells me you're gone—-*you don't exist anymore*
the *March Hare* offers me tea and tarts and tells me to get over
myself
but the *Knave of Hearts* steals them before I can indulge
I invite *Alice* to join me but she declines
tells me she'll be back tomorrow
and we'll try to find you——-*again*

The Mad Hatter: Have I gone mad?
Alice: I'm afraid so. You're entirely bonkers. But I'll tell you a
secret. All the best people are.

THAT'S (my) LIFE

I've been up and down
and over and out
and got kicked in the teeth
I've been good and holy
and evil and nasty
and made to feel beneath
but each time I felt like callin it quits
and leavin this earth
I picked myself up brushed myself off
and remembered my worth
my life
hell—it ain't been simple
many times I thought of packin it in
but instead I flashed my dimples
sometimes I find myself
flat on my back and fresh out of wine
and I wonder if I can even go on
cause I ain't got a dime
then I concentrate on the woman I am
and all I have to give
look in the mirror straighten my crown
and remember those I've outlived
my life
damn it sure goes by fast
it's lousy and hurtful
and beautiful and hopeful
and in case you should ask
I'm still standing and loving and funny as hell
I'm healthy and happy my mind's clear as a bell

but if I'm not filthy rich
by the end of the year
and not havin hot sex in the south hemisphere
I'm gonna shop till I drop
at the nearest huge mall
max out the credit cards and just have a ball
cause this life's too short
gotta live like I'm dyin
cause no matter what happens
I'll never stop tryin

> *"Who are you to judge the life I live?*
> I know I'm not perfect-and I don't live to be
> But before you start pointing fin-
gers——make sure your hands are clean
> Bob Marley

EPILOGUE

Well—here I am entering the twilight years—or so they say. While I'm not at all thrilled with growing older, it sure beats the hell out of the alternative. I've had a hell of a ride, that's for sure, and if I have my way (which I usually do) I've no intention of getting off at the next stop.

As I think back over the last 50 years or so, most of the special milestones in my life have been marked with music. Back in the 70's, I pretended to be a "hippie"! I wore the legendary bell bottoms, love beads and ironed my hair. I listened to Janis Joplin and The Who, smoked a little pot and fell asleep to John Lennon and Prince. I raised two healthy, active boys and gave up the pot—replaced it with an occasional "scotch on the rocks" and chose a more mellow musical entrance into the 80's.

At that point, I was all bout Billy Joel and Barbra Streisand. I'd practically OD on Earth Wind and Fire, and for those nights full of romance (that were few and far between) there was always Whitney Houston and Journey.

I put myself through nursing school, and fell in and out of love a few times—usually with the wrong man. I found that crying while listening to Lionel Ritchie and Phil Collins made things a bit easier. And there was always a group of friends that I could hit the disco scene with. There was nothing like a night of Donna Summer, Kool and the Gang and Gloria Gaynor to bring me back to life. *I will survive!*

In the 90's when my daughter was born, I became a believer in Chardonnay. With my family complete, I felt a sense of relief and comfort. I actually began to relax and who could help do just that when you heard Boyz to Men? There was always time for Sade, Backstreet

Boys and Mariah Carey! And what was better than a little music from Sesame Street and Barney?

I've done a complete 360 now, and the sweet sounds of Ella Fitzgerald, Frank Sinatra and Billie Holliday soothe me. Though most of that music was actually before my time (yes, I know I'm old enough to remember) I have always had a love for jazz and the big band era—perhaps because it reminds me of my dad. I've also learned to appreciate my family's musical talents more as I age! I have a nephew with an incredible voice, a great niece who can rock the house, and a sister who actually wrote a song. It's called the *Why Why Why* song—and though it'll never make the top 100 or Kasey Kasem's hit list, we sing it on the regular! We all love to sing and I must admit, we have more than a little musical ability!

I'm forever thankful for the music in my life. As I sit and sip my Chardonnay in the evening, I reflect on past decades. I listen to mostly theme songs now—Law and Order, Criminal minds and the Jeopardy tune—yet every once in a while, as I'm reminiscing about my younger years, I'll crank up the tunes, tease up the hair and dance with the dog!!! Ah—life is good!

Marianne

www.ingramcontent.com/pod-product-compliance
Lightning Source LLC
Chambersburg PA
CBHW071215130726

47998CB00002B/762